ISBN-10: 0-9993481-0-8

ISBN-13: 978-0-9993481-0-9

Distributed by:

CreateSpace
4900 LaCross Road
North Charleston, SC 29406
United States of America
Printed and bound in the USA

(No Pun Intended)

By St. Clair DeShong

To:

Elizabeth, who looked beyond the mangled words of my suffering and saw something positive in my writing; and who encouraged the beauty of expression, where others might have rebuffed my choice of words.

Thank You.

And

To:

Jessica, who opened the door to a brand new world of expression, which broke down the bars of the prison that trapped me within myself.

Thank You.

Thank You:

Calvin, Megan, Quincy, and Sabrina

TABLE OF CONTENTS

PREFACE

Song of Death

A bird upon a limb, humming a song
While children play their games of war and death.
A lioness lamenting— something's wrong.
Her cubs had vanished in one wink, one breath.
Like innocent bystanders being slain
In wars between the foolish and the proud,
The meek and mild must struggle to refrain
From hopeless sinners lurking in the crowd.
An eagle fights a crow over a fish.
I thought that there were more fish in the lake.
While one man smiles when crumbs are on his dish,
Another's vexed— he wants a bigger steak.
When one man cries because his brother's dead,
The ign'ant says, "One less mouth to be fed!"

1

YO' MAMMA
(WORDS)

"Sticks and stones may break my bones, but words will never hurt me."

— Unknown

Sticks and stones may break my bones
But words...they never hurt.
Or so some would say to try to downplay
What words are really worth.
As a man of few words,
I know just how much they matter.
Words can give life;
And words can cause a life to shatter,
Crumble and fall like tempered glass
Pitter-pattering on the past—
Yesterdays cast in memory's clay—
As spoken bullets hammer away.

Words.

Two words were always sure
To cause fists to fly,
No questions asked,
No need to apologize
Because no, I did not accept;

And no, I did not care why
You decided you were man enough
To cross that line:

Yo' mamma!

Stung like two bees shot from a gun,
Flung from a thirty-eight caliber revolver tongue.
I swung.
Reflexively.
Because the pain went to my brain
And affected me,
Effectively changing my destiny
For a moment,
'Cause anyone next to me
Potentially could have been beaten to death.
You see,
My mother was sacred,
And words spoken in hatred
Would not be allowed to taint her shrine.
If I could tell you how many times
Those words left me with tears in my eyes
Because someone stopped the fight
And I was not yet satisfied,
You'd probably think I was lying.
But in due time,
Those closest to me grew wise;
My mother was taboo,
Unless you wanted to die.
Word got around.

His mother's dead, stupid.

Yea, yo; his moms died.

But I was no fighter.
I was liquid butane trapped inside a lighter,
Peacefully inert until someone called forth my fire.
My desire

Was to set flames to the hem of their words
And watch as it burned and melted away the hurt.
But I didn't know how.
Sticks and stones would break my bones,
But words had shown such power!
Oh, how I would have rather to cower in a corner
And fade to death
Than hear one more person let it roll off their lips:
Little Motherless.
Little Motherless as they stared at me sadly,
Asking if that's the little boy for Angie.
The little boy who killed his mother.
The mother who died gladly.
Their words.
Their daggers.
They stabbed me.
And in my soul, I was angry.

Guilt grabbed me like a preprogrammed machine
Cold heartedly snatching a defective doll
From the assembly line.
Dejection dragged memories through my tender mind
Until I was convinced that the blame was mine.
I was the reason mommy died.
I was the reason daddy lost his smile.
The cursed child.
Disaster seemed to follow me like flies.
I was traumatized.
So, from a distance, I stared with jealous eyes,
Thinking how no one knew as well as I
How revolutionary it is
To long to linger by my mother's side;
But the revolution would not be televised
Because the transformation was taking place
On the inside.

Words.

Forlorn. Wistful. Melancholy. Depressed.

Sat on my chest like eggs in a nest
Waiting to hatch already full grown
As my unhappiness.
And every time one cracked,
I snapped...
Never too sure if this time would be the last.
The last dance with suicide.
I should have been dead so many times,
I began to think God punished me
By keeping me alive.
But all I wanted was to be loved.
All I wanted was to be hugged.
All I wanted was for someone to be proud of
Me.
Sticks and stones can't touch the soul,
But even unspoken words could gouge deep.
The silence articulated loudly
What I had already known.
Trees can't grow where seeds were never sown.
A mother's love is something I would never know,
I realized as I watched those who mothered me
Mother their own so lovingly;
And I would grow sad.
I never heard the words "I love you, son"
Until I was a man.
It seemed culturally illegal to be emotionally frank;
And frankly,
In my home, emotional transparency was banned.
But I needed that more than
A deaf man needs his hands.
Sitting with a psychiatrist
Was never part of the plan.

Words.

Words had gone from labeling me
To becoming who I am.
Little Motherless, now

Motherless Man.
"Sometimes I feel like a motherless child,"
My classmate sang mockingly,
Only to upset me.
And even though he had known me,
On that day he met me;
For I had kept me
In a bottle to prevent me
From doing something I would regret. See,
I needed an outlet;
Because from the outset,
It seemed I was destined to go crazy...
Multiple visits from a ghostly lady
Who eventually saved me
From the worst nightmare I ever had:
Feet stuck in dirty sand
As a host of demons ran after me fast.
She called to me, begging me to awaken;
And the closer they got, the more frantic she became.
But when I opened my eyes, the demons were still there,
So she reached out and touched me
And they all disappeared.
Then she too was gone,
And I was alone with my fear.
Sticks and stones may bruise the flesh,
But words are spiritual,
Strong.
I had to be spiritually strong,
Especially on birthdays, because I was torn.
Instead of lighting candles for me,
We lit candles for my mom.
To mourn.
But how long was I supposed to hold on?
I didn't know.
So at twenty-eight years old,
About to have kids of my own,
I broke up with a ghost!

Word.

I take nothing for granted.
My story happened just the way God planned it.
I had to be planted exactly where I landed,
To endure the pangs of becoming who I am.
I could have easily been a bandit
With all that I carried on my shoulders,
But I handled it.
God made me to handle it.
He gave me four mothers to compensate for the damages.
Four mothers to love me from four different angles.
Four hammers to shape me into God's candle
So that He could ignite my flame
And set me high up on a mantle.
Still, many will judge me, knowing very little of me.
No.
I am not perfect;
The only thing perfect is
His love towards me.
Sticks and stones may break my bones,
But they matter most when they're
Carving words into window panes of abandoned homes.
They matter most when they're
Marking graves of the lost but not forgotten souls.
But words become part of us.
And we exist in eternity.
That means words can last forever.
That's a lot longer than a cut can bleed.
So to have heard the few my mother spoke to me
Was like therapy;
And for me,
Is more than all the sticks and stones could ever be.
The sound of her voice is forever etched in my memory;
And her words have become like a sweet melody
That every now and then
Comes back to me.

2

MY MELODY

Melodies were made to be heard,
Whether played by instruments
Or crooned by birds.
They are streams
Flowing through the desert sand,
Bringing hope and life to whet the tongue
Of the thirsty land.
They are tunes
Tuned to the channel of emotions
Channeling through the you that's been going through
One or two things.
They are ripples
In a pond known as Time,
Sending waves of yesterdays through my mind...
So shall they ever sing of you,
A love sublime,
A peace in my soul,
A natural high.
Transpose your kiss
From C-minor
To A-sharp tingling bliss
In the major key of my heart
And resolve my sorrow.
Study music theory to compose E-E-Gs
That still can't capture God knows what

To label my thoughts of you.
I've fallen in love with you,
Fallen in love with loving you,
Forgotten how much I love you
And fallen in love with the memory
Of falling in love with you...
Only to rediscover you
And fall in love anew.
My melodies bear the essence of you,
So sweet that I can't stop listening,
So ingrained in me that without you,
A part of me is missing.
Minor dissonance between sweet notes
Only sing of a stronger connection,
And the circle of fifths
Will never be large enough
To contain our affection.
You are my melody,
My harmony,
My root.
You are my lips' blissful smile,
The joyful tears in my eyes.
The truth:
Your accidentals give purposeful ties
To what would otherwise be meaningless flaws,
Give cause to praise God
For the imperfections that are yours.
And my imperfections matter less because
Of you.
Because you are so great and
Your love is so true.
Because you are the best and
You make me better,
Too.
Because you are my melody,
And I will always sing of you.

3
WE

America has become
A society of mine, my, and me.
There is no more us and we,
Except in emergencies,
Where it's us against them and
We do not negotiate with terrorists.
"We" don't even mean anything
Politically.
We the People is a fading memory.
We the governed and they that govern
Are no longer a single entity.
Rules apply separately.
The constitution is now malleable
Except when malleability
Is an inconvenience
To those for whom the law is
Merely a formality.
Formally,
Society has been divided unequally
Into a small island
And an immeasurable sea.
And though they meet inextricably,
The land dwellers want nothing
To do with what they deem
Aquatic triviality.

4

TESTIFY

Only in Christ could a man's greatest downfall
Become his strongest asset.
Just imagine:

Bathed in sin
Like lumber in kerosene
As the devil holds the matches.
Down and out like fifty, love;
And it's game, set, and match.
You're the motherless child turned orphan,
Daily reminded that you're a bastard.
So, I ask:
When does it become routine
To daydream of yourself in a casket?
When does it become routine to
Live routinely as if life just happens?
When does fornication and love
Become as synonymous as bed and mattress?
When are yesterday's highs measured in ounces of vodka
And today's lows lost between moments of relapses?

When is enough ever enough
When enough never equals satisfaction?
I'll give you the answer.

When you realize that Jesus is Lord and master...
That you've been tried in the fire and found lacking.
When you realize that you're an unfinished sculpture
And all along you've been asking
For a master craftsman
To guide hammer and chisel into mind, body, and soul
Because years of foolish hacking
Have left you ugly.
When you concede that you are ugly.
That I am ugly.
When the me in the mirror hates me
Because of me
And yet He still loves me.
Grace and mercy poured upon me
Like hot butterscotch milk,
Melting away yesterdays like popsicle prisons
Beneath heated quilts
Even though I am not worthy.
But I am free.

Free to admit that I'm not worthy.
That I am but a shadow who long ago lost his sight
And through blind prayer, my savior heard me;
And through hearing Him,
I fumbled through darkness and stumbled into the light
To find that I couldn't be less deserving
Of Him.
But His eyes are on the sparrow.
His eyes are on the shadow
That in the light becomes light
So that darkness can't exist.
And the void in the dark where
The shadow once lived
Can only be filled by the light
That the shadow now is.

So, into the darkness I shine.
Familiar darkness,
Hear me testify of deliverance.
I, too, have sinned.
Repentance.
You, too, can win.
Assurance.
No matter how many times condemnation wears you out,
He is there to take you in.
There is no condemnation in Him.

And greater is He that is in you
Than he that is in them
That deride and condemn
Men who walk away from things
Like drug addiction
With only the conviction that
Jesus Christ can fix them.
And when Jesus fixes him,
He lifts his head:
A New Creation...
Resurrected from sin
With the strength of Christ within
So that the old sins remain old things.
They've passed away.
Drug addiction passed away.
Fornication passed away.
Prideful convictions passed away.
And he's no longer a castaway.
I am no longer a castaway.
You are no longer a castaway.
But you've tasted victory.
Tasted and seen the goodness of
The true and living king.
Now, your greatest downfall may be
A thing of the past,
But your testimony...
Your testimony is your greatest asset.
What He did for you,

He can do for others like you.

Don't be frightful.

A candle in the dark seems overpowered,
But from ten miles away it can be seen.
So let your testimony spark another
And another
And another
And see
How powerful a candle can be.
Testify.

5

FALSE FREEDOM

"Emancipate yourselves from mental slavery. None but ourselves can free our minds."

— *Bob Marley: Redemption Song*

This is my liberation
From the limitations of mental incarceration
Within a nation that incriminates them
That built history with blistering hands...
On knees, praying with the blistering pangs
Of a lineage that flowed with conviction in Kings.
Yes! We were born to be kings!
Yet, they stripped us of our names
And whipped us to do things—
Tried to kill our ancestry through lynching.
But my forefathers' blood remains within these veins:
The DNA of MLK and X,
Who marched for concepts
That made them martyrs for our people.
They marched,
But I crawl within my skin
Because we still can't see through
The false freedom that frees us to feel equal.
Meanwhile, three-fifths of a man
Becomes nearly forty percent of incarcerations[1]

And merely ten percent of college graduations.[2]
We've been balled and chained to a situation where
Black men don't feel like men
Because we can't help ourselves,
We can't help our children,
We can't help thinking the way we've been trained to think:
To hate them that share the same color skin
Because somehow, it's because of them
That we can't win.

Man, we're crawling.
We just crawled out from the Underground Railroad
Into the tunnel vision of drug addiction
And ruthless killing,
Praying while sinning
And selfish living.
I see now the world that I live in.
Live-out nannies caring for White women's children
While no one is at home to care for their own.
So, little Black girls
With a little too much freedom
To roam
Become former rape victims
With abortion syndrome.
And little Black boys get caught
Trying to survive the strife,
Living the self-fulfilling prophesy of
"Look to your left and look to your right:
One of you is not expected to see twenty-five
And the other is expected to do twenty-five to life." [3]

Now, what good is an absentee father?
They're setting the sons before they can rise.
So, why bother?
They're leaving an impression of depression
And "why bother?"
They're leaving them angry,
With no faith in our fathers.
No faith in Our Father.

6

HIS NAME
(COLLEGE GIRL)

For Nellie and Zinga:
Stay strong!

She drew his name. She drew his name as a burning flame amidst rose petals and shooting stars. And interrogations about constellations in the night sky left her lost. Who cares about Sagittarius when his Aquarius flows deliriously from tender lips to soulful bliss as a crush becomes precarious with nothing more than a soulful kiss? Fingertips tapped into her mind like Morse code, caressed her body and reprogrammed the source code. Two hundred miles away from home, so daddy can't be hurt by what he doesn't know. No. No more Sunday morning bible school and Pentecostal freak show. So, it's frat party body shots on Saturday nights and hookups with random people. Then, it's Sunday morning worship; call it porcelain praise: trying to piece together the past night from a Hennessey haze. She remembers how he stared from across the room, admiring the attire that daddy would not approve. But she worked it. Perfect. Gave him the shy eye service. Returned a stare that said: Who me? No, I'm a virgin.

The implications of her innocence infiltrated his inner senses. Sin drenched his need for repentance in his desire to penetrate her penitentiary. He was imprisoned in the weakness of his flesh. So he found strength in the fact that she appeared defenseless. But, she had him right where she wanted, like a pet in her palm, forgetting that the devil has a handsome charm. Mr. Joshua Lamar was a crush from afar, was a name she heard called on her dorm room floor, was the face in astronomy class next to the door and belonged to the boy who never noticed her before. But there he was chatting with Ms. Four Point Oh, Ms. Daughter-of-a-preacher, used to want to be a teacher, now dressed like a streaker, showing off her features. She used to be the best student; but now when she's called, she no longer knows the answers. She just sits and draws. She draws his name.

She called his name. She called his name loud enough to conceal her shame amidst expletives of Yes! and Baby! Dimmed the dorm room lights because in the dark of night, she might convince herself that this is love… maybe. It's crazy. Weeks ago, he was such a compassionate friend. She confided in him. He promised he would ask for her hand. "I'm a lady," she said. "Sex is a passionate thing. Let's just wait until we're married. We'll have lots of it then." Then… suddenly, he would leave hurriedly. No time to chit-chat. He said, "I be buried deep in my work all the time. Gotta focus on my future. Maybe when I make it big, I could shoot ya a line." He smiled and drifted away… became a face in the crowd for a couple of days. Until she saw him with Melissa in the back staircase and decided that she would rather have him than wait.

Wait… Wait! She heard the still soft whispering breath of her conscience as she tuned her hearing down to "Deaf." Scoured her soul until there was no guilt left and no soul to feel guilty that the wage is death for the sin that she commits as she forgets herself in the midst of making a mirage to camouflage the flesh, chasing what appears to be happiness. But the more she gets, the emptier she feels, and the more she wants. And the more she wants, the emptier she feels, and the more she feels like she can't be filled and she can't be healed; so she conceals her shame amidst expletives of Yes! and Baby! hoping that some day, it would feel like love… maybe. She called his name.

She cursed his name. She cursed his name in her thirst for pain, wishing she could wring his neck and burst his brain for leaving her with no one but herself to blame. She's barely past finals, but almost mid-term, feeling like what's inside her is more like a germ than a human. Should have thought about what she was doing when she parted her seas for the Moses wannabe who split at the first mention of the word pregnancy. Lost herself in the tendency to believe that he'd come around eventually, only to find that the sweet memories melted into thoughts of murder in the first degree. And the tender tune of denial changed its melody in due time, so she heard the song he sang was: that child is not mine… That child is NOT mine!

Anger for emphasis. Volume for truth. He re-wrote reality and left her confused and broken and hurting and emotionally abused, bursting with tears of: "What should I do? How could I go home with my body distorted? Daddy's gonna kill me, but I just can't abort it." So she stood upon the windowsill, four floors high, seeing no hope now through her forced-closed eyes; and her foremost cry was not for the Most High, but that four floors down, she would for sure die! Still, she bowed her head to pray; and in that very moment, she heard His loving voice, and she knew it was an omen: I am perfect. I am sovereign. And I make no mistakes. My child, you are forgiven; You shall not die this day. Now, go and be whole; turn away from your sins. And so, the preacher's daughter ceased to curse his name.

She praised His name.

7
The Ghost In The Machine
(PART I)

Setting: Near a well shaded park bench just outside the basketball courts of Lincoln Terrace Park in Brooklyn on a warm summer evening.

Character: Mr. Elijah: A tall, slim, gray-haired man with a gruff voice and a hoarse laugh.

Mr. Elijah's Narrative

Have you heard about the ghost in the machine?
I don't mean like *I, Robot* when Sonny had a dream.
I'm talking about knowledge corrupt,
Codes of conduct,
Propaganda,
And social constructs.
I'm talking about disinformation and miseducation.
I'm talking about Truth.
I call it a ghost because most of you can't see;
And whenever I talk about it, you say I'm crazy.
But I'd rather be institutionalized
Than to buy into this institution of
Modern-day slavery.

You got social security,
But that was originally an exclusion policy:
An extension of Jim Crow through politics.[4]

And welfare was designed to create poverty
Because you couldn't get a cent to put food on the table
As a Black family with a man at home who was able.[5]
But out in the real world,
They wouldn't throw a Black man a bone,
So the Black women dogged them out,
Made them leave home
So the children's bellies no loner had to groan.
They sold out to the government
Just to get that check;
So I guess that makes Uncle Sam a home wrecker.
He succeeded in destroying the Black family.
Yeah, they might give a little bit to the beneficiary,
But when you do the math, it looks more like trickery.
They raped your minds while you were asleep,
Impregnated you with ignorance,
And gave birth to stupidity.

You're walking the streets, thinking you're free;
But you're stuck in a prison you can't even see.
Bars built upon the dollar bills,
And I ain't talking about conspiracy theories.
This ain't got nothing to do with Illuminati and Free Masonry.
I'm talking about looking at life
From inside poverty,
Contemplating how long it's gonna be
Before you can live outside the walls of your
Maximum security neighborhood.
And no matter how you flip the script,
The boys in blue are no good,
Because they're there with the prejudice
That you're the criminal.
They're not there to protect you.
They're there to get you
Because the you next to you might have a pistol
That's really a wallet
That's really a symbol
For his awareness of the bars
From behind which he stares,

And this allusion to Truth fills their hearts
With fear,
So they must gun him down
And leave you there
As a reminder to those who want to escape.

So you sleepwalk awake,
Living the nightmare while chasing the American Dream
Without a Morpheus to come and set you free.
But the Truth is there,
This ghost in the machine.

8

FROM QUEENS TO BROOKLYN

Something special happened
Between Queens and Brooklyn.
It wasn't quite your swagger
Or the way you were looking;
Even though you filled my lungs with
A breath of fresh air
When I gasped at your dress
And the style of your hair.
I was compelled to compliment,
To say that I like.
And even though you didn't hear at first,
It's alright.
'Cause as we walked from the garden,
Arm around my arm,
Taking in the natural beauty and the calm
Of the man-made stream that ran beneath the bridge,
Thinking we should someday have one like it,
I felt this...
Faint, as if from a distance, this...
Vaguely familiar instance, this...

Not quite deja vu, this...
Not-quite-new-because-I-know-you, this...
Just feels right so why fight, why ask why... feeling.
But if I could measure that feeling,
Somehow quantify this thing,
It would be as a single feather
Plucked from a fledgling's wing.
Weightless.
And by comparison,
The light of your smile,
The gentle of your touch,
The comfort of your eyes...
Weighed so much that
I felt weightless by the time you parked the car.

Parallel parked your heart on the road of my soul
Where our destinies collided like a happy accident.
Head-on collision with love,
So sudden that it caught us by surprise.
And yet, slow enough for me to spend forever
Lost in your eyes.
Lost in the why,
The how...
The mathematically improbable probability
That this could be possible now.
Where now is the variable
Representing the aftermath of broken hearts
As alpha approaches chance
And the limit is undefined...
Stutter start.
False start.
Restart.
We start
As chance over time is overturned by
The Alpha and the Omega,
Who has no limit,
And the probability of two equaling one
As time approaches infinity
Is one.

God did it.
Whatever IT is...
This something that took them,
The her and the him,
To Love
From Queens to Brooklyn.

Just a taste of your cookie,
A sip of your wine,
An innocent dance as our hearts intertwined
Was enough to remind me
To never stop hoping,
'Cause when God makes a bond,
It can never be broken.
And God didn't just simply bind us.
He made love specifically for love to find us.
He made you for me and me for you
So that our love could be timeless.
And so that our love could glorify His name,
He blessed us in anticipation
That the devil would test us.
But just as the blood in my veins flow through my body,
The love I have for you flows through my soul.
And with God living within us, there is one thing I know:
Nothing will ever come between us,
Except death alone.

9

FATHER

Some men elevate themselves to a higher plane,
Riding the highs between love and hate,
Where fist meets face and souls become faceless,
Nameless.
And their tactics are shameless.
They redefine the fine line
So that they exist outside it,
And somewhere between face-bashing and
Verbal thrashing, they still turn up
Blameless
Because the only witness is a child
Who can't decide who they should blame less
For the inexplicable tears that rip holes
In the mind's eyes as memories transform into thoughts of
Maybe I should just die.
And these men, they smile.
Walk around with a sense of pride because
They tell themselves: I'm the man.
But they don't understand.
Every boy can grow up to be a man,

But not every man grows up to be a father.

Some men chase after cash, cars, and girls.
They lie, cheat, and steal
Trying to gain the whole world;
They lose their souls and their first-born sons,
Selling it all to the devil,
Trying to multiply their funds.
They keep figuring on biggering,
Just like the Onceler,
Cursing generations down to the great grandsons.
They wear clothes with names that are hard to pronounce
And drive cars with price tags to rival a house.
Age ain't but a number.
Sex ain't but a thing.
Five baby mommas that don't wear a ring.
Eight kids on child support
And they don't pay a thing!
And these men, they smile.
Walk around with a sense of pride because
They tell themselves: I'm the man.
But they don't understand.
Every boy can grow up to be a man,
But not every man grows up to be a father.

Father.
A father couldn't be farther from these men
Because the harder the father fathers,
The more the Father fathers him.
Leads him not into temptation
And delivers him from sin,
Renews his strength so he could mount up with wings
As eagles.
He's not just ordinary, people.
Faster than a speeding bullet.
More powerful than a locomotive.
Able to leap tall buildings in a single bound.
Take notice:
What greater love has a man than this:

To lay down his life for his friends?
A father would sacrifice his being
And forsake all things
For the sake of his wife and his offspring,
Which are his best friend and his children.
And this man, he smiles with love in his eyes.
No need to boast because his family is his pride,
And he tells himself:
I'm just a man.
See, he understands.
A young boy can grow up to be a man,
But men are mere mortals without the Father.

Father.
The thoughts of the Father couldn't be
Farther above the thoughts of men;
So he fathers them so they could be more like Him.
He teaches them how to tie their spiritual shoes,
Because fathering is a spiritual walk for men
And they have to understand their spiritual cues.
Chastise and not abuse.
Love and not misuse.
Seek the Father first and
All these things shall be added on to you!
And you can smile.
I can smile.
Walk around with a sense of pride
Because it's not by my strength but by
The strength of He that is greater than I.
Jehovah-Jireh. He will provide,
And all my needs He will supply.
That's why I will walk beside the still waters,
Never lay my hand on somebody's daughter,
Raise the sons better than I was brought up,
Be the father that I wasn't afforded...
Because I understand.
A boy can become a man by emulating men,
But men become fathers by emulating Him.

10

BULLIES IN HIDING

"We will have to repent in this generation not merely for the hateful words and actions of the bad people, but for the appalling silence of the good people." [6]

— *Dr. Martin Luther King, Jr.*

She took one glance at me and made up her mind
That I was too stupid to succeed
And just shy of wasting her time.
And though I didn't know how to be *that* dumb,
I sucked in my pride and just for fun,
Pretended to be too ignorant to mind
Her innuendos regarding my goals in life.
But while she served her condescension
With a side of pride,
Waving away my ambitions as if they were lies,
I analyzed,
Making note of how she rolled her eyes
At my expressed desire to become a doctor.
And perhaps it shocked her
When she finally pulled up my file
And saw a Brooklyn Tech grad
With grades Deans list high,
But I wouldn't know
Because she barely even batted an eye.
Instead, she adjusted her style,

Trying subtlety for a while.

Have you considered other career options?

She smiled.

But she had already revealed herself by that time,

And I had already rejected her input in my life;

So we were stalemate:

She, another racist

Trying to hide behind a position

While dispensing blind hatred

To those who fit the profile...

And I, a few years ahead of my time

Because experience brought wisdom early in life,

Just a tad on the intellectual side,

And enough people skills to recognize

When a smile isn't a smile.

After all, it wasn't the first time I encountered her type.

Every young, Black male growing up in Crown Heights

In the 90's had to have known what it was like.

Being Black was like having a bounty on your head;

And as far as the cops were concerned,

You were already dead.

A corpse with no future.

You just didn't know it yet.

And harassment to them was an ongoing bet.

Like: fifty bucks says I can make this one shake...

Rough him up, pat him down, and put a gun in his face.

But the situation rarely ever played out that way

Because there are some things

Innocent people don't tolerate.

So when ignorance meets indignation,

It's a bomb you can't diffuse;

And it typically ends with the Post or Daily News

Having a third page article about abuse:

Young Black Teen Hospitalized By Six Cops, White; Grandmother Dies.[7]

That was *my* headline.

That was *my* cousin left with only slits for eyes,

Face so swollen you couldn't even recognize him.

That was *my* grandmother who raised me

When I was a child.
My family broken.
My family crying.
And as per protocol, the judge wouldn't indict
Despite witness after witness who testified.
And the salt in the wound was that after the trial,
The same cops came and found us,
My cousin and I,
In the park near our house
To harass us
And smile.

I realized this:
Bullies come in all different shapes and sizes.
Uniformed racists are bullies in hiding.
They wear their positions and fake the smiles
Until the moment to hate openly arises.
Then, they're "just doing their jobs,"
No matter how outrageous;
And the ecosystem of the country makes it
Environmentally friendly for camouflaged hatred
To prey on the infrastructure of the nation.
To the government, the whole matter is laissez-faire.
Let dog eat dog;
It's a jungle out there.
But it's only possible because of ignorance and fear.
Misconceptions among those too far removed to care.
They see nuance statistics [8]
That shed no light
On causality, relationships, affects, or plights.
They don't see how negativity within social constructs
Give rise to long-term negative social conduct
Like ebb and flow, push and shove;
The hatred in the air can't precipitate as love.
Think about this: stop-and-frisk
Produced more criminals than the Bloods and the Crips;
And most of them haven't ever been arrested yet.
Hatred begets more hatred;
And hatred is worse yet when hatred is educated:

Systematic oppression integrated
Into a culture of vultures masquerading
As doves.
But when you push a man's head
Below the water long enough,
You'll see how fiercely he fights
To bring it up.

11

WOMANIZER

He wears his liquor like expensive cologne.

Just enough to leave a lingering scent on his clothes.
Eyes bloodshot
From a decade of voluntary inhalation of marijuana smoke.
No joke.
Attitude like a raging bull strung out on cocaine.
Not enough sense left to talk logic back into his brain.
He's a runaway train.
Can't decide if his wife and kids are trapped.
Locked inside one of the cars, or tied to the tracks.
Either way, the rails are running out fast,
And sooner or later this train is going to crash.
The children are mannequins with faces painted in laughter,
Ashamed and afraid but can't hide the strings of his wrath.
In his anger, he puppeteers a dance of terror.
And in their wincing and crying still can't see his error.
In the mirror,
He is a god with his biceps flexed and twitching pecs
As his wife hides under the blanket,

Trying to avoid what's next.
He will never beg for sex.
His pride will never let him.
And the stories of headaches and fatigue only upset him.
He's a married man and
Therefore, it's his to take.
So he takes it
And she dares not utter the word rape,
Lest she pays with the beauty of her face.

He wears his liquor like expensive cologne.

Just enough to leave a lingering scent on his clothes.
Tears explode
From his eyes in apologetic woe
Because the slap from last night broke the zygomatic bone.
No joke.
The doctor says she's lucky;
She could have lost her sight.
He implores her to try to get that man
Out of her life.
But she insists
That she was being really clumsy last night—
That she tripped on the top stair
And rolled down the whole flight.
Meanwhile, as the hard mask she was prescribed to wear
Begins to sweat on her face,
She could just barely hear
Above her imaginings of running away with the two kids,
The drone of him declaring
How much better he's going to live...
How much more he's going to change.
But in her absentminded daze, she fails to reply.
Fails to accept his apology for the third straight time.
His impatience gets the best of him,
And in the blink of an eye,
Her head hits the wall and she's gasping for life.
The warmth of his palms against her neck is fading fast,

And the last thing she hears is
Something about not respecting him as a man.

He wears his liquor like expensive cologne.

Just enough to leave a lingering scent on his clothes.
Eyes transfixed on the IV hose,
Contemplating how to silence his wife by overdose.
No joke.
Dr. Edwards enters, stethoscope in hand,
Reviled by the repose of such a vitriolic man...
Bold enough to beat his wife unconscious
With his bare hands
And complain
That the doctors aren't doing the best they can
Because she's incoherent and unable to stand.
Damn.
With feigned concern, he inquires about her state. .
Just a few moments longer could have been too late.
You see, the brain needs oxygen; and when you suffocate...
Well, you know the story.
Let's wait 'til she awakes.
But before she could focus the blur out of her eyes,
Two officers appear as the doc steps aside.
"Sir, can I ask you to please step outside?
We have some questions to ask you concerning your wife."
Fear is not an option.
Profanities fly.
But obscenities cannot obscure the fact
That he's out of time.
Arrested for assault and attempted murder,
He's looking at a minimum ten years this time.
Unless she once again throws out the charges
For fear that he'd do far less time on a plea bargain,
And then come find her in a timely manner
And take what it appears he's always been after:
Her life.

12

THE GHOST IN THE MACHINE
(PART II)

Setting: SGO rally, front steps of the library at Brooklyn College on a cool and breezy September afternoon.

Character: Marlon, an articulate though slightly overweight male of approximately twenty years old, with a fuzzy chin and a small afro.

Marlon's Speech

I'll be your Neo, your bender of spoons;

I'll show you that what really has to bend is you.

Flex your minds like uterine contractions

And give birth to a revolution,

Because we've been in labor for four centuries.

Pregnant with the hope of being treated equally.

We've long been behind enemy lines,

Whether it's the 36th parallel,

The poverty line,

Or the line of fire.

Yet, we sell our souls to the cheapest buyer,

Spending tuition money

On prison attire

So our pants could sag

And we could brag who's flier.

Meanwhile, we collectively fail to aspire

To achieve higher.

The situation is dire.

We've upgraded our nooses to liquors and loosies,
Tech nines, and technology so exclusive
That we don't even know what to do with it.
Sex-texting like it's the next best thing
Since sliced bread;
Quoting Lil' Wayne, but we don't have a clue
What Christ said.
We're chained to the ghetto
By the Beamer, Benz, or Bentley...
Spending cash so fast that when we die,
The bank is empty.
So our children get nothing—
No chance at being wealthy.
The struggle is prolonged;
Poverty becomes a disease,
And we're the least healthy.

We've re-written our genes so that we're poverty prone.
We're now susceptible to strokes, diabetes, and loans.
Or should I say debt?
Because for reasons unknown,
We have no money, but we're buying new cars and homes!
They've pulled the wool over our eyes.
We believe the lies.
We think we're making more money,
When inflation is on the rise.
We're trying to get better jobs,
But unemployment is sky high.
We're the first to apply and the last to get hired;
On the top of the list when it's time to get fired.
We complain,
But I say again:
The situation is dire.
We've got high school diplomas.
They've got Master's and higher!
It's not a lack of ability.
It's a lack of desire.
It's a slow but systematic destruction
Of our whole, entire race;

And I'll tell you why.

The children are the future,
And the government is wise;
They're brainwashing the children
And corrupting their minds.
Disinformation and miseducation.
Columbus was a hero, and
Slavery ended with the Emancipation Proclamation.[9]
They control the media and our children's education.
And we're too lazy to rectify the situation.
Our sons are at the parks with their hopes and aspirations
Of being rappers
And sports entertainment's next generation.
And we didn't go to college,
So we don't have the information
To tell them the real Truth about this lying nation.
Knowledge is power, and the children... they are weak!
They're at war, and they've been blinded;
They can't win 'cause they can't see!

They can't see
That they're chasing jobs and not careers.
They're dropping out of college
Because they have the wrong ideas.
They're fed fashion and technology,
And their minds have been prepared that
They gotta have it now;
Can't wait another year.
And as parents, we look at this,
And we don't even care.
Because they have what we didn't have,
We think they're doing fair.
But when we go to doctors,
The doctors think "next"
Because all they know about us
Is what they read in some text.
The politicians ignore us,
So we don't have a voice.

We vote against abortion
And they vote pro choice!
The scientists are working in the fields they are told
Because the government is funding,
And without it, they fold.
So who's looking out for the interests of the Blacks
Back in our neighborhoods
With the liquor stores, the guns, and the crack?
All we have are the pastors,
Who try to give us just enough Faith
So we don't kill ourselves long enough to escape.
Funny thing is:
When we make it, we forget where we're from.
Are the memories so bad
That we wash our hands and say we're done?

We've got to help our people.
Knowledge is the key.
Tell them the Truth;
Show them the ghost in the machine.
It's time to wake up; we already had the dream.
Dr. King has been gone for over half a century.
We're no longer fighting people, but principalities
And powers in high places.
Knowledge is what we need.
Not a 10% graduation rate.[10]
Read!
Tell the children the Truth.
Help them to succeed.
Stop living for today as if you're dying tomorrow,
Because all they will inherit are
Our sins and our sorrows.
We need doctors, lawyers, scientists, priests...
Not volunteers for jail 'cause they can't make ends meet.
Not voluntary slaves who believe that they're free.
Ignorance is a plague.
The Truth shall set you free.

13

(No Pun Intended)

Dedicated to:

Amadou Diallo, Sean Bell, Trayvon Martin, Michael Brown, William Chapman II, Eric Garner, Sandra Bland, Freddie Gray, Akai Gurley, Alton Sterling and the many others who have been killed.

They're *killing* us (No pun intended).
There's no statistic that can render it
Clearly enough through the misdirection[11] that
Black is offensive across the nation.
The boldness and pride with which we blithely
Approach a white society
Still trying to hide oppression
Everywhere from classrooms to coffee shops[12]
Like moonshine in the prohibition
Is like Bitrex in their thoughts.
They half expected us to fearfully submit
To what they see as rightful dominion[13]
And live as pets or perhaps even as children,
Obedient to their flimsy and ever-changing,
Sometimes violently infected with hatred,
Sometimes callously tolerant,
But rarely genuinely loving
Will.

So, they're *killing* us (No pun intended).

In broad daylight and out in the open.
Telling us it is for our own benefit,
As if to say:
Spare the rod and spoil the children.
Spare the bullet, spoil the city.
Lamentation for weed-smoking, gun-toting Niggers
Is silly.
It's not like they have
Children,
Wives,
Purpose,
Futures.
It's not like it matters
That the false accusers
Are also the ones pulling the triggers:
Power abusers.
They have become
Judges,
Jurors, and
Executioners.
And the justice system fails
To uphold the constitution[14]
In its efforts to reconstitute us.

Yeah. They're *killing* us (No pun intended).
For the same crimes as them,
We get harsher sentences.[15]
They harass and arrest us for minor offenses
And tarnish our names so that those intending
To hire us in the future would tend against it.
Meanwhile, White males with multiple arrests
Can go on to become men of great success.[16]
Obviously, there is no disconnect.
To say that all men are equal is disrespect.
Three-fifths of a man does not a whole man make
Simply because someone grew a conscience
And decided to say so.
In the minds of those whose hearts are not changed,
Evil is without cause and wickedness without blame.

Ask yourself why the media does not portray
Cops murdering unarmed White men
And getting away.

Because they're killing *us* (No pun intended).
Intentionally by accident like fake pretending.
Mistakenly building prisons to put our men in
While simultaneously neglecting the system
That educates our children.[17]
As if it were never their intention to
Fill the very same prisons
With the very same children,
Who suffer a lack of wisdom
From a watered-down education
That leaves them non-complacent
And acutely aware of the
Acute chronic hatred
That hangs over their nation like
A planet-sized spaceship
While their government downright denies
The ongoing invasion.
It's just our overactive imaginations.
Something like when we wander across the imaginary borders
Between our corner of squalor
And their bourgeois quarters
And we ask for directions
Because we're genuinely lost
And they over-actively imagine not to hear our voices
Or see our faces
Or care for our causes.
In the 21st century, this still goes on.
Racism has grown like fresh flowers
In the same old lawn.

And just like in centuries gone,
They're *killing* us.

(No pun intended)

14

EVENTUALLY MUST COME

"Let me urge you to be sane and rational. Eventually segregation…will pass away. Eventually." [18]

— *Martin Luther King Jr.*

"punk
n. …An often aggressive or violent young man…
v. …To act in a cowardly manner…"

— *The American Heritage Dictionary of the English Language, 5th ed.*

Punk cop got a gun on his hip.
Trigger finger got an itch.
So he shoots another Black man
Down.
Punk judge got a grudge,
Got a chip on his shoulder
'Cause a chick,
When he showed her love,
Shut him down…
For a Black guy.
Now he's that guy.
Dishing out racism
Like it's pot pie.
Let the punk cop go.
Now the punk cop knows
He can get away
With murdering a Black guy.

How many times?
How many times does an

Unarmed Black man
Have to be killed
Before the system finally convicts them...
Racist cops...
Lock them up in the jail?
How is every situation the same:
White cop, Black male, and the claim
That he had a gun or
He was violent?
And when the truth comes out,
It is silenced!
Autopsies sealed by a judge.[19]
Dash cams, body cams all fudged.[20]
Video evidence leaked to the news
And when brought to the trial,
The judge says you can't use it.
Why?
Because it's on YouTube.
It's too mainstream
For a fair trial to ensue.[21]
That's a load of B. S.
We want justice.
They're killing us at will.
We've had enough of this.

What if Black cops started shooting
White men?
Went into White neighborhoods
And harassed them?
There's a level of absurdity
Just to mention it,
'Cause everybody knows
They'd probably get life sentences.
There'd be an uproar.
And then an outpour of
Prudently penned legislature to end
What they're now sure is
"Racism within the P. D.
And will not be tolerated...

Must stop immediately."
Where is our outcry
From those who sit on high,
Up there on Capital Hill
On either side of the isle?
They've closed their eyes.
It's almost like they despise us.
They sit idly by while
We die and protest, and
We die and protest
As they watch us in silence!

Yet they have rallies for
The rights of the gays as
The blood of young Black men
Seeps into the pavement.[22]
Wow! What a powerful statement!
But we are patiently losing our patience.
We've been waiting for change
In our own situations.
But change doesn't always happen.
Sometimes you have to make it.
And we will make it
One way or another.
Our "eventually" must come,
My sisters and brothers.

15

SONRÍA
(SPANGLISH)

Santería and Rosaries
Santa María and Poetry
La chica bonita
With the white flowers
In her hair...
Sonría!

Besos! Besos para mí
The scent of love y dulces
Su cara in my memory
Dígame how you do it

Hace llover en mi alma
Cuando hay teardrops
In your eyes
Cuando estas triste,
Mi corazón, it dies

La chica bonita
With the white flowers,
Sonría!
Because you y la tuya
Son la vida mía

16

THIS AIN'T
HOLLYWOOD

In slow motion, the flock of doves takes to flight. The tropical backdrop is bathed in rich sunlight, blurred as the camera pans to the right to reveal a sky that is more blue than white. The powerful thrusts of wings appear as a graceful dance, with a scatter of doves that must have been choreographed. I laugh in my mind and ask, "What if real life were just like that?" This would be my dramatic close-up with eyes hot with tears, pure love written there, as off in the distance somewhere, you appear strolling towards me in a long, flowing dress that still hugs your hips and accents your breasts. It would be green, no less... the color that suits you best. And somehow, a plain gold chain would glisten around your neck, and your hair would suddenly move under the wind's caress. Focus. Zoom. Your lips aglow with a Cucumber Melon sheen, teeth white as snow, eyes bright as diamonds with glimmer and gleam, and two dimpled cheeks with a smile in between. But this ain't Hollywood.

Our love can't be scripted. No pause and replay if you blinked and you missed it. No cameras roll, action! First Kiss, Take Two. This is one chance, one time. No "Cut!" and redo. This is real life, and Hollywood could never measure up... could never quite capture the essence of our love no matter how good the make-up or how many doves taking off in slow-mo as you come strolling up. 'Cause the look in your eyes can't be rendered on screen. Cameras simply can't fathom the soul that

I see! And the hammer of my heart, the rush in my veins when I lay eyes on you or hear mentioned your name can't be duplicated. Something always remains... too TV, too twice removed, too grounded in fiction, too not-quite-true. And not to mention the touch of you, the feel of your luscious lips doing what they do, arousing a passion so deep and so true that each kiss brings it out like it's brand spanking new. Hollywood doesn't have a clue! And the sweet scent of your skin like fresh paint on my memory's canvas is a portrait that eludes every camera angle and leaves films feeling anguished because your scent speaks volumes, and they don't know the language. No... this ain't Hollywood.

Choir voices sforzando dissonant chords as we argue, and the camera shakes just enough to make it hard to focus on the who; but hearing the what is still only a part of the view. Frustrations flare as words fail to express that this moment does not amount to unhappiness, that in spite of the pain on my countenance, I love you no less. Even the "uncut" director's cut leaves the truth in the gray. And the would-be commentary has nothing to say about the fact that every night when I lay down to pray, I thank God for the blessings that He sent my way when He knitted our souls on that September day. This ain't some cheesy screenplay with over-the-top romance. *The Notebook* and *Gone With The Wind* have no chance. This ain't Hollywood. Reality is a different program. It's the simple things... the things not worthy of soap operas; no close-up of a gun on the night stand, next to the Vodka; no violins as close friends advise you to see a doctor 'cause the rash that you have means *sorry, man; she gotcha!* No dolly-zoom when Maury booms, "You are NOT the father!" That's a different type of drama; I can NOT be bothered. This is the too complex to explain, but we understand love... this is the unconditional type, lay my life in your hands love... this is the semper fi, never lie, do or die love... this is the stick by your side through the rain or the shine love. This... God made this and He said it was good. Whatever *this* is... this ain't Hollywood.

17

THE GHOST IN THE
MACHINE
(PART III)

"Train up a child in the way he should go, And when he is old he will not depart from it"

— Proverbs 22:6

Setting: *Living room of Jude's house on Super Bowl Sunday; halftime. Jude and six friends debate over the targeted audience of a commercial that appeared humorous to all except Jude.*

Character: *Jude, a high school history teacher and avid reader. He has long locks and wears glasses.*

Jude's Rationale

The strategy is simple; or so I was told:
Get 'em while they're young
And you'll have 'em when they're old.
So says the sex industry
And every cigarette brand,
Every liquor company,
And the leaders of this land.
They target our children— an ingenious plan:
Destroy the Black youth, and you
Destroy the Black man!
It wouldn't be the first time
The leaders tried genocide
For fear that their slaves would
Some day unite and rise.
Remove the veil from your eyes!
What does history say?
Pharaoh killed the Hebrews' sons
In Moses' day!

Millennia of change, and
Things still stay the same;
They want us to remain
Eating from the palm of their hands.
They have centuries of information
Being passed through generations!
They are the esoteric!
We've heard but a fraction of the conversation.
But we don't need a Rosetta stone
For the full translation...
Knowledge and Truth will bring us Revelation!

And Time will bring us
The crown of our ancestors,
For we are a chosen people.[23]
God himself handpicked us!
We were kings in our own land,
Chiefs of mighty tribes.
We were stripped of our humanity,
Beaten, and told lies.
Starved of our own culture,
Hated, and deprived.
Three-fifths of a man, they said;
Who are they to decide?
All we had were the spirituals
We sung in the fields,
But Faith is dangerous weapon
If you know how it's wielded.
Faith gave us Hope,
And Hope is hard to kill
'Cause you can't kill a man
If you can't kill his will.
Three-fifths or not:
In the coffin or the jail,
Our Faith will send a mountain on its way
Like it was mail.
Faith started the Church;
The Church started the schools.[24]
They might have made the game,

But God made the rules.
And all along, they knew that
We were destined to succeed,
So they lied and denied a whole race
The right to read.
Because Knowledge is power;
And their power made them greedy;
So they built themselves a government,
A well-oiled machine,
Designed to keep power in the hands of the elite
While always diligently alluding to democracy.

But there's a flaw in the system,
A ghost in the machine.
The Truth is written there,
And in fact, had always been.
And we've been too distracted
With survival
To ever see.
We're volunteering to be slaves
After fighting to be free.
We're being led astray
'Cause we're too ignorant to lead.
We're buying into what we're told
Because we're too lazy to read.
I'm talking about
Knowledge corrupt,
Codes of conduct,
Propaganda, and
Social constructs.
A subtle but intricate system.
An answer
To the Knowledge
That has recently risen amongst us.
Take heed; this is a war,
And the enemy is keen.
Truth is the answer...
The ghost in the machine.

18

RIDDLED WITH THE SIGNS

"The more things change, the more they stay the same."

— *French Proverb*

Edifice riddled with signs of the baroque:
Flying buttresses and demons upon their posts.
Charged with the mission of chasing away the ghosts,
But the spirit of racism reigns coast to coast.
The blood of the innocent cries out the most,
Like a telltale heart underneath the floor posts.
But where's the confession that beckons to be told
By the thugs in uniform, channeling the Jim Crow?
Bullets for a noose.
Nothing lost in translation.
Patrol cars for slave ships.
Prisons for plantations.
The terminology has evolved with the times,
But like the edifice the people are
Still riddled with the signs.
Justice flaunts her pride as she saunters by.
Unarmed Black men, murdered, give a desperate cry;
But she pretends not to hear them and averts her eyes.
She pretends not to *hear* them and averts her eyes!

Edifice riddled with signs of the baroque:
Vaulted ceilings fail to uplift a lost hope.
Frustration fuels fury, and fires ignite the focus
Of news and talk shows that paint with broad strokes
Dichromatic stories of Niggers in dark cloaks
On a law-breaking quest to upset the status quo.
They say,
"Death to them all!
Society's better without them.
As for the cops, applaud.
They are just and devout men."
Who will shed a tear for the likes of Freddie Gray?
And if Eric Garner wasn't selling loosies,
He'd be here today.
That's what people say...
What ignorant people say...
What those who see Black and White
And not wrong and right say.
They fail to consider the punishment versus the crime.
Just like the edifice, they are
Still riddled with the signs.
Instead, they seek to separate a mother from her child
For flogging him in public to instill a life lesson.[25]
It's abuse!
As if they don't discipline their own.
The hypocrites!
Talk about salt in the wound!

Edifice riddled with signs of the baroque
As complex statuettes hide the lies they evoke.
Like death depicted in a masterful work,
Never alluding to the terror
That would bathe a North Carolina church
In blood.
A place supposed to house God's love,
Invaded by the hatred of a racist thug.
And while many cry out for justice,
Some secretly call him just.
Confederate flags fly in favor of an era

When Blacks were hung from trees
As a sign of terror
To those who dared believe
That freedom would reign
In a land intended for the White man
And his Negro slaves.
Worshipers slaughtered even as they prayed.
One alone left alive to tell the tale.
Run Nigger run! I could hear the gunman say
With a smug grin as he pretends to take aim at his prey.
Such men we sit next to on the bus,
And they look at us with a smile,
But inside...inside they are
Still riddled with the signs.
I ask why.
Why are the things concerning Blacks so lopsided?
The Gammadion cross has become
One of the worlds most offensive signs;
But where the southern cross is concerned,
It is merely a blurred line.

19

ASHAMED
(MY PEOPLE)

*"If my people, which are called by my name, shall humble themselves,
and pray, and seek my face, and turn from their wicked ways; then will I
hear from heaven, and will forgive their sin, and will heal their land."*

— *2 Chronicles 7:14*

Generation next:
Defined by drugs, alcohol, and sex.
They are rock stars
Before pubic hairs and breasts.
Public display of aggression,
As profanities chin check the elders in attendance
Who fear to object.
They stare in silence and accept
The death of respect in the progeny.
What used to look like fine mahogany
Appears to be nothing more than birch:
Stripped to the core, base and without worth.
I am ashamed of my people.

My own race engaged in embarrassing acts
That fuel stereotypes about the young and Black.
This is far more significant
Than a mere generation gap.
This is the manifestation of an utter lack
Of interest in the facts.

They're riding slack as history blurs past;
And no one cares enough to even glance back.
Identity has become synonymous with the latest fad.
So, they've become synonymous with the latest brands.
They've become synonymous with a movement
To be called gays and not fags;
And as another White cop murders another unarmed Black man,
They fail to understand.
True indignation is replaced
By a generic incarnation of frustration
Built upon crowd dynamics:
Multiple iterations of "enough is enough"
Copied and pasted onto raw mechanics,
Like mindless robots operating on learned habits.
Pavlov's dogs.
It's tragic.
I'm ashamed of my people.

Somewhere beyond thug life and club life,
Where it's so "turnt up" in their love life
That they reject God just because they love life
And would rather have sex than have love like
The kind when Jesus Christ died to give us life,
They've gone to live in damnation,
Saying sin is just imagination,
The delusive creation of some distant dictator
Dreaming of world domination.
Let's call it what it is:
They're worshipping Satan.
They fill their blunts, their bottles, their syringes
With enough lies
To blow the door to reality off the hinges,
And they shoot up,
Hooked on self gratification
While cops shoot us
By the hundreds and laugh in our faces
From behind the safety of the knowledge
That this broken nation's broken system
Will exculpate them.

I am ashamed of my people.

There's nothing wrong with aspiring to better yourself,
But you're not a better you if you're never yourself.
False images like mirages in the desert of your soul
Where false idols are the sand that you grip but can't hold;
But false pride won't let you let go,
So the sun rises in the east and sets in the west
As your compass continues to point north
And you somehow continue to be lost.
How much education will it take
Until you're smart enough
To see the prison you're living in?
How many have to be murdered
Before you call it genocide?
How many times do you have to willingly
Submit to injustice
Before you call it giving in?
How long must you keep your eyes closed
Before you're considered blind?
Fitness is defined as the ability of a group
To reach adulthood and successfully reproduce.
Now, when they're killing our male youths,
It's not a far cry to suggest that
Exactly what they're trying to do
Is reduce our population by reducing our fitness
And subjugate our people through fear and oppression.
I've witnessed the hatred of racism evolve
From dumb prejudice to sophisticated injustice.
Meanwhile, my people die for want of wisdom.
I am ashamed.

But if my people who are called by my name would humble themselves and pray,
and seek God's face, and turn from their wicked ways, then will they hear from
heaven...

20

ISMS
(LETTER OF REGRET)

I will purge my soul
With the wine of drunken words
Poured into this virtual cup
Of confessionism and contextual isms
Of logic and illogical emotions
With their emotional rhythms
Motioning me to give
Life to my struggle,
Life to my pain,
Life to the death inside
Beckoning to insanity,
Life to my shame.

The recurrence of recent events
Projected onto my retina
Through the recollection of what was retained
Is driving me insane:
Rewind and play again and again,
And nothing has changed;
All is the same.

I soiled your soul,
Stained your psyche
With the blood of my sins;
And it's quite likely that this stain
Just might be the nail in the coffin,
The cake's frosting,
The guilt in my throat that keeps me coughing,
Coughing,
Talking to myself in the dead of night,
Conversing with the demons of hindsight,
Saying that if I knew, I might, and
You're right.

But rewind and play again and again
And there I am doing the same thing;
Nothing has changed.
My heart bellows thick smoke
From the fire burning inside my soul,
And I'm choking on emotions never foretold
Because the chill that kept me cold
Forced me to withhold
As if silence is still a virtue;
But how virtuous was my speech
When I did unleash
The truth that hurt you?
Rewind and play again in slow motion:
Ice cream, light beam, sounds of the ocean…
Tokens of a time too tragic to tarry on,
But too meaningful to move on
And not bother to carry on.
Slower still as time kills me
With acceptance in you eyes.

Fast forward to the moment when I dangled in denial,
Faced the truth with blind sight
To the error of my crime,
And pleaded with innocence
Though I was guilty at the trial.
Now I'm facing the sentence:

I-wish-I-Knew-ism,
Blue-ism,
Life-without-you-ism,
And I skip another euphemism
To say that I messed up;
And that's true-ism.
So I start a new rhythm.
A-boom-boom klat; A-klat a-boom klat.
But the beats in my head can't drown out the facts.
So the beat in my heart just loops and plays back,
"It's more than 'I like you a lot;' don't say that."

But the recent events reverberate in my mind
And I hear myself repeating it every single time.
I like you a lot.
Rewind and play again and again;
It doesn't change.
I like you a lot;
That's what I hear myself saying.
Now I'm facing the sentence:
You not staying,
Me wishing you did day out and day in,
Wondering if things would change
If I did some more praying
And spoke it into being
In Jesus' name.

Instead, I'm here with just my drunken words:
Life to my pain,
Life to the death inside of me,
Life to my shame
As I jealously view the memory of our intimacies
To the melody of your intimating that this never will be;
And I intimately explore the intricacies
Of another intimate He replacing me.
Such is my sentence:
I'm-missing-you-ism,
Knowing-that-there-is-no-replacing-you-ism,
Shoulda-coulda-but-I-wish-our-love-grew-ism.

That's true-ism.
But I had to start a new rhythm.
So I wrote you a song
(Well, it's still in the making)
Because I think of you,
Eyes closed or in the waking.
I'm not faking or saying this to say things.
On the scale of what you mean to me,
You out-do the ratings.
But I digress;
The point of this letter in general was to say this:
I doubt genies exist,
But if I had one wish…

21

MY MIDIAN
(MOSES)

Even as

The breath-snatching ignominy

Of cruel conviction

Crippled my cruising feet

Beneath the burning affliction of regret in my Midian:

A shame black as obsidian,

Transfiguring hope into derision

Exacerbated by division in the psyche,

A mission to despise me

By me,

A collision between

The must live me and

The must die me,

A confrontation with Death

So untimely that time itself had to be stymied

So that I could find me

A burning bush,

A talking flame,

A holy of holies to call my name

And remind me

That I walk on sacred ground...
Even so, I found
That there is no sweeter sound
Than the whisper of God
As His love abounds to me:
Forgiveness, deliverance, purpose.

Even as
The blood-stained shackled remembrances
Of a time not so distant passed
Dance upon the blackened stage
In my memory's latest act...
Dance as demons cast to play puppet masters,
Pulling plasters from deep-seated disasters
Hand-crafted by the wicked heart that bashes
The caverns of my soul
And echoes a laugh-less madness
That could only be consoled
By the clasp and fold of hands that know
From practice
How prayer captures my master's glances
And affords me second chances
Because the fact is:
Long ago, my Lord took my lashes
And was pierced in His side by the lances...
Even as they dance,
His mercy,
His grace,
His hand is
Reaching out for me.

Even as
The vicious plague
Of a carnal flesh
Seeks to undermine the Savior's touch
Like Pharaoh refusing to acquiesce
In light of a greater force,
The cost of my eternity
Will not be the first-born sons.

My metaphorical window
Is drenched in the Lamb's blood.
I have learned to stand upon the rock
In the midst of sinking sand.
I've learned to face adversities
The size of Red Seas with
Just what's in my hand.
I've learned that knowledge
Is not always what you understand,
But sometimes what you believe,
And in rare cases what you can't.
That's why you have to have faith
In order to see the promised land.
Idol-worshiping in the wilderness
While seeing the works of His hand
Is not an option,
Is not a part of the plan...
Even as my flesh seeks to undermine,
I've learned in time to deny myself and
Trust in God.

22

BOTH SIDES

Building up the temple, building up
the temple, building up the temple
of the Lord. Boys want to help us.
Girls want to help us...

Echoes of sadness ripple in the dark as elevated trains thunder through the night. Broken promises shatter time and awaken prostitutes and prisoners. Somewhere, lonely comforts a mother of four who grow bitter with hunger and the unspoken anticipation of seeing a father who went to the store last week Thursday. Cold fright lay frozen on the faces of those too fragile for the far too frequent ejaculations of gunfire and chilling cries at night. Hope has gone to hide in the dust-covered textbooks of dilapidated classrooms, at the fingertips and out of reach of the illiterate. Respect is hard to come by for the endangered educator who dares to still care in the modern era of the extinction of education in the hood, caught in the crosshairs of powerless profanities and prideful perversions from those ignorant enough to believe that education equals embarrassment equals enslavement to a hidden force. Dreams dissolve in the solution of societal silence regarding the isolation, injustice, and ignoring of a people plagued by poverty, problems, and prejudice. Whom do we say have sinned?

Jesus wants me for a sun beam,
a sun beam, a sun beam. Jesus
wants me for a sun beam. I'll be
a sun beam for him...

Across the train tracks, the buildings shrink and the houses grow. The streets have exchanged the scent of cannabis and booze for a new cologne. Gentrification is complete here, and the upper echelon discretely pen their unwritten legislation of legal segregation in the language of economics to reestablish the status quo. Status shows in the makes and models that align driveways and extravagant homes bearing stickers in windows and staked signs in lawns that say: African Detection Technology. Schools don the best selections of latest edition texts and six-figure anti-affirmative action checks. Someone has to pay to build the bridge from inner city slums to modest, maximum security bunks. Uncle Sam has to collect interest off the principle on Welfare. Or did you think it was free? The children of the privileged bear witness and testify to the wind about the sickness that plagues those with the darker skin; and they keep them at a distance... don't want to catch their lack of prosperity, their cannibalistic mentality. In their prayers, they pray like the Pharisee, thanking God for not letting them be as the publican.

Joshua fought the battle of Jericho,
Jericho, Jericho. Joshua fought the
battle of Jericho, and the walls came
tumbling down...

Out of the ashes of hatred and sin shall arise a flaming phoenix of ignominy. And it shall lay waste to Babylon, a land that gave birth to its own irony. Philosophy and ideology eradicate what institutions have erected. The rich, the poor, the young, the old, the wise... are confounded by foolish things. Fortresses stand refortified in post Al-Qaeda pride as We The People crumble beneath the weight of tortured souls. But what is a nation if not its people? What is a church if not its people? Tortured souls fill our homes from window to peep hole as we fill pews and pray prayers that only reach the steeple. Our Jerusalem is weakened. Her walls are broken. And the saints? They are weeping and gnashing teeth. The world mocks: Where is your God? Call Him louder. Peradventure, He sleeps! But our God doesn't slumber. It is we who have allowed sin to tear asunder our body the temple, our city the church; we, who are called to do the Lord's work. So, who will rebuild His temple? Who will rebuild the walls? Who will save the children and the mother of four? Who will educate the ignorant and give wisdom to the wise? And who will pray for the rich, in whom no salvation lies?

Building up the temple, building up
the temple, building up the temple
of the Lord...

23

COME. SEE.

Come.
Walk with me on a journey and see
How we went from Niggers
To saying Nigga so freely.
"My Nigga!"
As if Nigga has no meaning.
But Nigga means everything,
Because the freedom to say Nigga freely
Still does not free me.
It doesn't free you.
It carries the pain of our people.
And it's lethal
Because we're killing the memory
Of what we've been through.
We force-feed this poison to the younger generation,
Then turn our heads as they start regurgitating:
Nigga this; and
Nigga that;
Forgetting that only yesterday a Nigger would be slapped
Just for speaking out of turn.

We haven't learned.
Grown men were treated like little boys.
Go fetch, Boy!
Don't you look *me* in the eye, Boy!
Duddn't it feel good to drive *my* Rolls Royce, Boy?

I am a Boy
In this broken world,
Speaking to deaf ears because no one has heard:
Mental slavery is passed on like a dominant gene;
And for the non-biologists,
Let me explain what I mean.
The lack of knowledge leaves the children blind,
So they've evolved to see without their minds.
They've evolved to penis in vagina
On kitchen tables, breaking china,
Ejaculating ignorance so timeless
That it consumes *their* children
And leaves *them* mindless—
Lost in a world of domestic violence,
Poverty,
Illiteracy, and
Excess crime...
With racism so clear
That you can't even find it.
Trapped inside their own neighborhoods,
Thinking home is a destination.
Home is a journey dictated by gentrification;
And when it's time to move,
They still have to pack up and leave the plantation.
They ask,
"What plantation? I don't see any fields."
In the concrete jungle, do we live amongst the trees?
We cut ourselves from one another,
And the future bleeds
Because our vision is coagulated;
We're stuck on re... re... re...

Repeat the mistakes of our past.

Relive the mistakes of our dads.
Retain the hate that we have,
Which we were given without direction.
So, we direct it at the mirror's reflection,
Because He is Me and I am Them
And They hate Me because I am Him.
But in the end, it all boils down to the same thing.
Self-hatred.
I hate myself.
I hate my skin.
I hate the fact that I can't win.
And so we all lose
Because we all choose
To compete against each other
Instead of uniting like the Jews.
Fools.
Men are fools;
And I am a man.
So, foolishly, here I am,
Heart on sleeves in this broken world,
Trying to teach to those who won't learn.
But if I don't try, I'm responsible,
As are those who are knowledgeable
And fail to combat the unconscionable.
I will not mourn my people
While they live like zombies,
Dead to the Truth.
I will live
And breathe life into the lungs of the dying youth,
Because the children are the future.
Come.
See.

24

POVERTY RISING

"The paradox of education is precisely this - that as one begins to become conscious one begins to examine the society in which he is being educated." [27]

— *James A. Baldwin*

Hear the growl of the bellies of hungry children
Like thunder across a hopeless sky.
Poverty rising:
The unsettled dust of the inner city, climbing,
Threatening to obscure the view from on high.
The affluent float by
In search of where next to gentrify
As basketball bricks on crate
And excitement subsides.
Foul.
Lines blur between extortion and capitalism
As tenants get evicted
Under the guise of renovation
So that rent could triple.[28]
Legalism is lost on them,
For they know not their rights.
Three decades and three generations
Relocate almost overnight.
Just as the hood was getting a little quieter,
Just as there were less drugs and less gunfire,
Just as the playground finally got back the swings
And the basketball courts

Were finally getting back the rims...
Just as the White people started moving in,
The Black folks are forced into a corner of squalor again.
Suddenly, where the dark skinned ones used to live
Is prime real estate.
Their three hundred thousand dollar home
Is now valued at eight,
And nothing has changed but the furniture and the paint.
Statistically, the change is far from being in the gray.
It's one shade lighter than eminent domain and
Two significant figures away from stone cold racism.

Hear the growl of the bellies of hungry children
Like thunder across a hopeless sky.
Poverty rising:
The unsettled dust of decrepit classrooms, thickening,
Threatening to darken the veil of ignorance
Covering their eyes.
Opportunity passes by,
Unnoticed by those too busy to avert their attention
From struggling to survive.
Rent to pay.
Bills to pay.
Diapers to buy.
And when you carry the ones,
The math just doesn't seem right.
Down at the bottom of the barrel,
Trickle-down is still a theory,
And whether the economy is in the red or the black,
The future outlook is dreary.
How can you climb the proverbial ladder
When you need a staircase to reach the rung?
Unseen hands of the esoteric
Orchestrate measures to keep you down:
Legislature penned in a dialect
You need a law degree to translate,
Prejudiced real estate agents who sell
Only to those who know the secret handshake,
Benefits and privileges

For those of the right skin shade.
Racism is now an intellectual game
Subtly to be played,
Fixed from the outset,
Referees all paid.

Hear the growl.
Hear their bellies like thunder.
Poverty like a disease.
Symptoms include
Shame, despair, inexplicable anger.
Who will explain to the children
What they're feeling and why?
Who will tell them that their anger
Does not originate from inside?
External factors mutate little Black boys
Like delicate eggs becoming hard boiled.
They live in a hot water society,
Being cooked alive psychologically and emotionally.
They are one step removed from actually being in the fire,
Incessantly under fire.
Generation after generation, racism spreads like wildfire.
As more Blacks attend college,
Bigger degrees are required
For jobs that barely pay enough for families to get by on.[29]
And those that can't afford the cost of higher learning
Become negatively skewed stats society uses to burn them.
Sixty percent of Black males drop out of college.[30]
Well, eighty percent of those
Almost didn't go to start with.
It was only for the experience right from the beginning:
A semester or a year liberated from their prisons.
And many return with hatred,
Because they see the true face
Of their neighborhoods as cages
Disguised as homely places.
So now they're burning with a thirst they can't quench
Because freedom costs dollars
And it doesn't make sense.

25

PORTRAIT

Allow me to paint a portrait
Of a naked poor kid
Standing in the rain by the orchids.
He looks as if he's finally lost it,
As if he's reached the brink of insanity
And crossed it.
The bitter stroke of my brush contorts it,
But the analysts agree:
He's holding something amorphous.
The radiant light from this object is offset
By the pallid gray sky and the shadowy porches
Just beyond his fortress of deep blue orchids
That luminesce like flowery torches.
But his fiery eyes outshine burning crosses
Set ablaze by KKK forces...
Cowards in masks,
Who never wait for bricks to crash
Through windows
Before vanishing on horses.
He might be living a nightmare

As he turns and tosses
In his fear of being just another Negro boy
In just another Negro family
Being tortured.

Fast forward to the 21st century.
Drop him into modern society
And watch as confusion grips him quietly.
White cops beat and kill Negroes at will;
But Blacks don't have to walk three miles over the hill
To go to a segregated school.
They can find one right around the corner.
Almost all Black from teacher to child,
With a severe lack of books and school supplies—
The only thing missing are the "Colored Only" signs.
Neighborhoods are still color coded,
And the ones occupied by Blacks are still the most eroded.
Is this freedom?
White women hold hands with Black men, and
Black women hold hands with White men.
But White society still discriminates against
Their dark-skinned mulatto children.
Watch how it treats them!
Is this freedom?
Black dads now college grads
Still can't get jobs the White man has
Because they're overqualified, under-experienced,
Black.
But they can vote now.
Is this freedom?
It appears the KKK have put away their masks
And have put out ads welcoming Blacks,
Yet rednecks with guns and confederate flags
Walk into prayer meetings at will and kill Black pastors.
Is this freedom?

Tears fill his eyes as the world shimmers and gleams
Behind the knowledge that a dream and half a century
Couldn't change a thing.

New York City in twenty fifteen
Is just as bad as nineteen fifty Montgomery,
It seems.
But he hasn't forgotten the thing he holds...
The amorphous thing that all but glows.
Faith.
Faith could change the world,
And love is the medium through which it flows.
Then will the rough places be made smooth
And the high places be made low.

"This is the faith that I go back to the South with... With this faith we will be able to transform the jangling discords of our nation into a beautiful symphony of brotherhood."

~ Martin Luther King, Jr.

26

POLITICALLY INCORRECT

"politically incorrect
adjective
        :[not] conforming to a particular socio-political ideology or
point of view, especially to a liberal point of view concerned with pro-
moting tolerance and avoiding offence in matters of race, class, gender,
and sexual orientation."

— *The American Heritage Dictionary of the English Language, 5th ed.*

To stand alone,
Transfixed somewhere
Between the ambiguities of temptation and
The complexities of self denial,
As the government puts religion on trial
And basic constitutional rights are denied
Is like standing before Nebuchadnezzar
As he prepares the fire,
Believing only that God is on my side.
For, you encourage me to reject my God and
Embrace your "politically correct" ideologies;
But, there is nothing politically correct about your
Hypocrisy.
You keep trying to convince me
That my Christianity is inappropriate for
Reality,
Humanity,
Sanity.
You say Christianity is fanaticism.
Emotional irrationalism.

Yet your embrace all philosophy
Fails to embrace me,
Us,
Him.
You seem only capable of
Embracing
All
Sin.

But, it's not politically correct
To directly address your dogma,
Your bigotry,
Your sanctimony and say:
That's one *ugly* baby!
And maybe, just maybe,
If you weren't so busy trying to justify your wrongs,
You would be able to acknowledge the truth
Instead of wishing me gone.
But I will stay,
And I will say what you say:
Free country;
Freedom of speech;
Man, your baby is *ugly*!
I can't even begin to pretend to not notice.
Racism, wrapped in a blanket in your stroller.
You nourish it, nurture it, and teach it politics.
Then, when it's mature, you don't even acknowledge it.
Blind to a hatred that is indiscriminate.
It is anti-Christian, anti-Semitic.
It is anti -Muslim, -Hindu, -Buddhist.
It is anti-immigrant nationalistic,
Atheist-minded Darwinistic.
It is disestablishmentarian, which is
Antigovernment, anarchistic.
And you say it has the right
To be all this while you deny me the rights
The constitution lists.[31]
This is what your definition of democracy is.
Democracy for all.

Who oppose it, kill them.
Democracy for all who oppose if it kills them.
You reserve the right to police and protect,
So you reserve our rights...
To police and protect.

Yeah. It's not politically correct
To stare at your murder crusade
To promote "democracy,"
Your capitalist taxonomy for legally enforced poverty,
Your White supremacy,
Black power,
Free Masonry philosophy and say:
That's one *ugly* baby!
But while you throw out labels trying to redefine me,
I leak into your mainstream;
You can't confine me.
I am between the pop-cultured minds
Distracted by Miley, Justin and Rhianna
While you feed them timely doses of controversy
As the economy stymies
And the Bill of Rights becomes fools' promises in writing.
The constitution has expired and our leaders are smiling.
This is the U.S. of all who accepts it blindly...
One nation, under God.
In God we trust.
As long as God cannot govern those who govern us.

But is it politically correct
For me to even suggest that God exists?
Because then your baby,
Love me or hate me,
Becomes
Ugly!

27

WHAT THEY SAID
(MY DADDY)

"jumby

A ghost or evil spirit among American and West Indian Blacks."

— *The Oxford English Dictionary, 2nd ed.*

They said Daddy was a rolling stone.
They said Daddy used to roll in... stoned.
How would I know?
I didn't live with him.
Never got to sit with him.
In all the memories I have,
I was a kid with him.
And even though they were few and far between,
If you look... Oh!
There goes me!
I got a smile on my face:
Just grinning from ear to ear,
'Cause there was just this one thing
When Daddy was there.
When I would see him from way back there,
I used to run with my arms stretched way up here,
Screaming, "Daddy!"
And Daddy never ran because Daddy was a man,
But Daddy used to stoop down and
Scoop me in his hands.

And you could feel the love
In every one of Daddy's hugs;
And I didn't care that they said that
Daddy was on drugs.

They said Daddy was a "Cocaine Jumby,"
But even in the way that he spoke he loved me.
This is "My Youth-man," he dubbed me
And spoke proudly any time he was speaking of me.
And they said...
What they said, I wouldn't repeat
'Cause in my whole entire life,
My Daddy never beat me,
Except that one time
When I said what they said
And I saw my Daddy's eyes turn watery red.
I'll never forget.
And yet, they said Daddy was the best.
Daddy was a carpenter far beyond the rest.
So when I walked,
Holding on to Daddy's nail-pierced hands,
Covered in plasters from where he slipped with the hammer,
I was glad.
This was "My Daddy."

Daddy was a giant;
He wasn't just a man.
He carried me on his shoulders,
High above the land.
And up there...
Up there, I wasn't just a child.
I was the prince of a king respected far and wide.
But time... time tainted his reputation
As the issues of life cursed yet another generation.
Another father-son relation stolen by Satan.
And they said...
And they said...
And they said...

And as I laid upon a park bench
One September night,
Homeless and cold,
I could almost recite what they said,
Wishing that I was dead,
Longing for mom and dad.
Maybe if I had a father when I was ten
And I was the best at dancing and my so-called friends
Used tease and tell me ballet is not for men...
Maybe things would have been different then.
Maybe if I had a Daddy
When I was running track and field
And I was breaking all the records
For my school's track team
But nobody in my family was there to see...
Maybe Daddy would have supported me.
What about when I was old enough
To have a girl on my arm,
Handsome as ever,
With the brains and the charm?
Maybe Daddy would have sat me down
And gave me a warning:
Son, I am the Evening,
And you are the Morning;
And if you make me Night,
There will be weeping and mourning;
So think about this
When you're holding your darling and
Hold her just far enough to keep on longing.

Longing became bitterness,
Bitterness became anger,
Anger became depression, and
I became a stranger brushing his teeth
In a college campus bathroom,
Embarrassed that my clothes were a week old
And I was not groomed.
Eyes lowered when better men
Walked in to pee,

Ashamed that when they looked at me,

They saw me.

Dirty.

Sin-drenched.

Dripping in heresy.

Past so dark, neither the therapy

Nor the medicine could remedy.

Tipped back a bottle of Agomelatine

And laid down to die alone in my sleep.

I woke up the next day,

Angry

Because I woke up the next day.

So I brushed it off and

I made up my mind

That I would never sit in the chair another time,

That I would never again medicate

To alter the chemistry of my mind.

I turned to my heavenly father

Who kept me alive and said:

You want me to be here,

So you be my guide!

And for some strange reason,

The hopeless sinner who barely believed

In a higher being

Found himself hanging with the Christians.

Found himself gravitating to their club,

Where they said:

God is good.

And:

God is love.

They said that He is the cornerstone.

They said that He rose on the third day

When the angel rolled away the stone.

How would I know?

All my memories were painted with a palate of sin,

But if you look... Oh!

Here I am.

I got a smile on my face:

Just grinning from ear to ear,
'Cause there is just this one thing
When Daddy is near.
I could run into his arms with my burdens and cares,
Whisper my secrets softly in His ears.
And with the strength of His love,
He would wipe away my fears;
And it doesn't matter that they said that
He isn't really there.

Daddy is the son of God;
He isn't just a man.
He carries me on His shoulders...
Makes me better than I am.
And up there...
Up there, I'm not just a child.
I am heir and joint heirs with the Prince of Peace. I...
Couldn't care less about time, because in my father's eyes,
I was worth dying for long before there was I;
And time couldn't change His mind,
Couldn't change His reputation.
That's why when they say:
He's just a figment of your imagination...
He's just an emotional sensation...
He's just a prophet, like Mohammed...
I say: Wait, man!

You don't know my Daddy like I do.
My father is not confined to my bible.
When I laid upon a park bench
One September night,
Homeless and cold,
I didn't have to recite a psalm or
A verse from the holy scripture,
My Daddy stepped in and changed the whole picture.
You weren't there in the dark
When I committed suicide and
My Daddy stepped in like a flaming fire,
Lifted me from the darkness and talked with me,

Then He ordered my steps and still walked with me.

You don't know the extent of His grace and mercy towards me.

Matter of fact, you don't know my Daddy;

So don't talk badly about "My Daddy."

My Daddy... He's the best!

He's a carpenter, far beyond ALL the rest.

So when I walk, holding on to Daddy's nail-pierced hands,

You can look at me and see

Why I am

Who I am.

It doesn't matter what they said!

I love my Daddy!

28

SKIN

"Can the Ethiopian change his skin, or the leopard his spots? then may ye also do good, that are accustomed to do evil."

— *Jeremiah 13:23*

You might have heard of Alexandria.
You might have learned of Egypt.
But before the Pharos and the pyramids,
Africa was not void of meaning.[32]
So why has Black history been
Relegated to twenty-eight days
And twenty-nine days each leap year?
Why does Black history begin with
The Atlantic Slave Trade
And end with
Poverty and welfare?
Whose story is that?
So... pre Egypt, there were no Blacks?
And since then, there's only
Slavery, oppression, and poverty?
Let's step back.

Africa had always been a world power,[33]
But you'll never hear that in a school.
They don't teach it.

They just allude to the wealth and the gold
When they talk about the
White men who sailed there to reach it.[34]
As if there weren't any Africans there...
No dark-skinned men who possessed all this wealth.
Somehow, history has made them all disappear
And convinced us there's nothing to tell!
No, they don't talk about Kush,
The Mali, the Ghana, the Axum...
The thriving empires and dynasties of the Black ones.[35]
While Europeans faced extinction by the plague,
Africa was hustling and bustling with trade.[36]
It was nothing like the picture we are shown:
Half naked men with spears tipped with stone,
Crude bows and arrows and noses pierced by bone—
Cavemen living in a world not their own.
I'm not saying the tribes didn't exist,
But that African civilization was
Far beyond this.

There was eco-social hierarchy, much like in Rome,
And many of the wealthy had slaves of their own.[37]
Now, now.
Hold on.
This wasn't slavery like the slavery *you* know;
Not that less-than-a-man, getting branded and sold;
Not that blister your hands working 'til you die,
Lose your feet if you roam;
Not that whip to your back if the slave driver
Doesn't like what you've done.
This was more like indentured servitude...
A poorer man working for lodging and food,
Or temporary ownership until he could pay his dues
Or save enough to make it through.
But these are things they neglect to tell you.

Instead, they try to
Rewrite history through the lens
That all our greatest achievements

Began with White men.
The Carthaginians: White.
The Nubians: White.
Ethiopians, Egyptians, and Libyans: White.[38]
But as they try to rape us and blatantly deny it,
The historical and DNA evidence [39] say,
"Yeah, right!"
It's just more of the same tactics
They've been using for so long;
Like when they raid and steal our music
And claim it as their own.[40]
Like when they assimilate our culture [41]
And call it theirs alone.
It's a superiority complex
Built on the fear that we are better
And that if given the chance, we'll prove it;
So, they'd kill us before they let us.[42]
But why does it matter?
Can the Ethiopian change his skin,
Or the leopard his spots?
Then will they do good,
Who are accustomed to doing evil.
But redemption is written
Into the persecution of our people.
For centuries, we've been hated
And oppressed because of our skin.
But the secret they're silently wallowing in
Will come out in the end:
That they've been wanting to be us since it all began,
And one of the things coveted most
Is the color of our
Skin.[43]

29

THE FORECAST
(THE PROPHECY)

"Yet with a steady beat,
Have not our weary feet
Come to the place for which our fathers sighed?" [44]

— *James W. Johnson: Lift Every Voice and Sing*

The twenty-first century is slated to see a marked increase in racism, with the degree of hatred expected to reach sadism. An explosion of interracial relationships and a high pressure system that promotes anti-Negro sentiment while steadily encouraging the tolerance of anti-Negro epithets will result in severe turbulence between those whose pigment of skin is dark and their melanin-deficient counterparts who, given the choice, more closely identify with the part of themselves that isn't vilified, rejected, and constantly subjected to strategic oppression. History will become historically irrelevant because segregation and slavery were against the Blacks and Black is a thing of the past and any empathy for such horrific acts is fading fast. Like, why are we still holding on to that? I mean, even our president was Black! *Come on!* It doesn't get much better than that.

There will be no light shed on the prejudiced. Ignorance will continue to veil the ever-distant holy grail called Justice as the victims of a system designed to protect them continue to wrestle with it's alter ego, which alters the appearance of evil to extend the shelf life of the placebo they've labeled Freedom so that the socio-economically enslaved can continue believing that struggling from paycheck to paycheck to pay bills and to pay rent while incessantly chasing a mirage of happiness in the form of the American Dream is what it means to be free. They are as tortured souls in the bowels of hell, sentenced to an eternal quest for equality in a land not their own, under the rule of a people determined to never relinquish control to the formerly owned, "less than full blown" man. Every ounce of success shall be met with iron-fisted hands clenching tight to higher positions of authority, better promotions in the company, better real estate for sale in better neighborhoods, higher education without the risk of going broke. And it's unfortunate that the ever more elegantly intricate obstacle courses that they intercalate in the societal mainframe to intentionally obfuscate and frustrate those whose hair isn't naturally straight and whose complexion isn't naturally pale become as phantoms for a people who *must* be insane, always babbling about a "system" and accusing a "man."

There will be decades of drought in which love will not reign in the hearts of children lost in wicked ways, raised to reject brethren because of race and to see shades of skin in colors of hate. They will be confounded by the growing rate of interracial offspring because they lack the understanding that love knows no boundaries. Yet their indiscriminate need to discriminate will inevitably lead these same offspring to disseminate hate. Hate for the Black roots from which stems their discord between real self, ideal self, projected self, and the distorted reflection society projects on the self they struggle to nurture to health. They will fail to comprehend until they understand the spiritual nature of their self-contempt. The external race wars will rage within them like flames feeding feverishly on oxygen, consuming them in subconscious guilt like the earth crying out for Able's blood spilt by Cain; and the derision and disdain for their own flesh and blood will pain them enough for them to take notice that something... some ambiguous and yet ubiquitous *something* is wrong.

There will be no epiphany. No grand moment when axon terminals burst open in a symphony of neurotransmitters chemically inducing wisdom in synapses to suddenly usher forth change. It will be as anticlimactic as someone saying: haven't we had enough of this race thing? And those who themselves have been afflicted by the controversy of being controversially in between will agree because they recognize that some time ago they had already begun to see themselves as either both or neither. Because we are not our skin color. We are not the texture of our hair. Our potential isn't measured in college acceptances; neither is our success measured in dollars per year. Our beauty is not skin deep. And as bleak as our past may appear to be, failure will never be our legacy. So, whether you beat it into us or burn it into our skin, pour it into our cups and force us to drink, we shall overcome. We are made in the image and likeness of God. And some day, *they* will look in the mirror and see *us* and say: *I* am fearfully and wonderfully made.

NOTES

1. *Morris, Monique W.. Black Stats: African Americans by the Numbers in the Twenty-first Century. The New Press, 2014, pp 74.*

   13th. Dir. Ava DuVernay. Netflix, 2016. Film, 1:23:02-1:23:50.

2. *Morris, pp 21.*

3. *13th. Dir. Ava DuVernay. Netflix, 2016. Film, 1:23:02-1:23:50.*

4. *Neubeck, Kenneth J, and Noel A. Cazenave. Welfare Racism: Playing the Race Card Against America's Poor. Routledge, 2001, pp 46–48; pp 54–57.*

   Katznelson, Ira. When Affirmative Action was White: An Untold History of Racial Inequality in Twentieth-Century America. Norton & Company, Inc., 2006, pp 142-143.

5. *Neubeck and Cazenave, pp 60.*

6. *Oxford Dictionary of Quotations, 8th ed. Edited by Elizabeth Knowles. Oxford University Press, 2014, pp 450*

7. *Not actual title. Original article was in New York Post. See 1995 Archives.*

8. *"Nuance Statistics" are statistics with correlations, which are intentionally misinterpreted to "show" causal relationships. For example, a stat showing a dramatic increase in the arrests of minorities can be manipulated to "show" a dramatic increase in crime by that demographic. In reality, the increase in arrests may be due entirely to the implementation of racially biased stop-and-frisk policies and reflect no real impact on crime rates (assuming there was a change in crime rates at all).*

9. *Alexander, Michelle. The New Jim Crow: Mass Incarceration in the Age of Colorblindness. The New Press, 2012, pp 31–32; pp 185–200;pp 234.*

   Blackmon, Douglas A.. Slavery by Another Name: The Re-Enslavement of Black Americans from the Civil War to World War II. Anchor Books, 2009, pp 111; pp 120-122.

   13th. Dir. Ava DuVernay. Netflix, 2016. Film, 1:24:40-1:25:40

10. *Morris, pp 21.*

11. *Alexander, pp 128-139.*

    Blackmon, pp 237-242.

    Neubeck & Cazenave, pp 204-210.

12. *Alexander, pp 45-48.*

    Katznelson, pp 162.

    Neubeck & Cazenave, pp 140-143.

13. *Diop, Cheik A.. The African Origin of Civilization: Myth or Reality. Edited and translated by Mercer Cook. Lawrence Hill & Co., 1974, pp 23-28, pp70-72, pp 132-133.*

    Blackmon, pp 236.

14. *The 4th, 5th, 6th, and 8th amendments of the U.S. Constitution provide certain rights that are consistently denied to Blacks and other minorities. Particularly: protection against illegal searches and seizures; protection against the deprivation of life, liberty, or property without due process of law; the right to a speedy and public trial with a neutral jury and with an attorney; and protection against cruel and unusual punishment.*

Alexander, pp 61-69.

13th. Dir. Ava DuVernay. Netflix, 2016. Film, 1:09:10-1:14:20.

15. *Morris, pp 75-79.*

16. *13th. Dir. Ava DuVernay. Netflix, 2016. Film, 1:16:03-1:18:00.*

Alexander, pp 191-192.

Pager, Devah, Bruce Western, and Bart Bonikowski. "Discrimination in Low-Wage Labor Market: A Field Experiment." American Sociological Review, 2009, Vol. 74 (October: 777-799).

17. *Lawrence, Sarah, and Jeremy Travis. The New Landscape of Imprisonment: Mapping America's Prison Expansion. Urban Institute, 2004, pp 8-10, pp 20-30.*

Stullich, Stephanie, Ivy Morgan, and Oliver Schack. State and Local Expenditures on Corrections and Education: A Brief from the U.S. Department of Education, Policy and Program Studies Service. July 2016, pp 1, pp 5-13.

18. *A Special Presentation of American Experience: Eyes on the Prize: America's Civil Rights Movement, 1954-1985, PBS.org. Retrieved 2008. Documentary, Part 1: Awakenings 19544-1956, 41:26-41:40.*

19. *The Associated Press. "Judge Has Sealed Alton Sterling's Autopsy Report, Coroner Says." NBC News, 2 August 2016.*

20. *Dash Cams and body cams are useless when they are turned off (as in the case of Paul O'Neal), or when the actions in question occur off screen (as in the case of Sandra Bland).*

21. *Frieden, Jonathan D., and Leigh M. Murray. "The Admissibility of Electronic Evidence Under the Federal Rules of Evidence". Richmond Journal of Law and Technology, vol. 17, iss. 2, 2011, pp 3-4.*

Some states have laws in place requiring a court order for the release and use of law enforcement videos.

22. *In the wake of a string of high profile killings of unarmed Black men by White police officers (Eric Garner in July of 2014, Mike Brown in August 2014, and Akai Gurley in November 2014), an outraged Black community awaited justice from America's legal system. Instead, they got the death of Freddie Gray in April of 2015; and instead of passing legislature to combat what appeared to be the indiscriminate slaughter of Black men, the Supreme Court handed down legislature to legalize same sex marriages in America in June of 2015.*

23. *Diop, pp 45-49, pp75-84, pp 105-106.*

24. *Woodson, Carter Godwin. The Mis-Education of the Negro. Digireads.com Publishing, 2016, pp 25.*

Woodson, Carter Godwin. The History of the Negro Church. The Associated Publishers, 1921, pp 167-169, pp 202-219.

25. *Bello, Marisol. "Mom of the Year? Baltimore Mom Isn't a Hero at All." USA Today, 29 April 2015. www.usatoday.com*

26. Wright, Richard. *Native Son.* Perennial, 2003, pp 47-48.

27. Baldwin, James. *"A Talk to Teachers." The Price of the Ticket: Collected Non-Fiction 1948-1985.* St. Martin's Press, 1985, pp 325-332.

28. Powell, John A., and Marguerite L. Spencer. *"Giving Them the Old One-Two: Gentrification and the K.O. of Impoverished Urban Dwellers of Color." Berkeley Law Scholarship Repository,* vol. 46 Howard L.J. 433, 2002, pp 436-454, pp 458-465.

29. Michel, Lawrence, and Jared Bernstein and Sylvia Allegretto. *The State of Working America 2006/2007.* ILR Press, 2007, pp 1-13, pp 19-22, pp 31-34.

30. Matthews-Whetstone, Rayna, and Joyce A. Scott. *"Factors affecting bachelor's degree completion among Black males with prior attrition." Research in Higher Educational Journal,* Volume 28, May 2015, pp 2-3.

31. Whitehead, John W., and Steve H. Aden. *Forfeiting "Enduring Freedom" for "Homeland Security": A Constitutional Analysis of the USA PATRIOT Act and the Justice Department's Anti-Terrorism Initiatives. American University Law Review,* vol. 51. The Rutherford Institute, 2002, pp 1083-1085, pp 1094-1132.

32. Diop, pp 1-2, pp 67-69, pp 147-152.

33. Burstein, Stanley. *Ancient African Civilizations.* 1st ed. Weiner, Markus Publishers, Inc. 2009, pp 3, pp 8-17

    Heinemann Educational Books. *General History of Africa IV: Africa from the 12th to the 16th Century.* Edited by D. T. Niane. United Nations Educational, Scientific, and Cultural Organization,1984, pp 614.

    Levtzion, Nehemiah, and Jay Spaulding. *Medieval West Africa: Views from Arab Scholars and Merchants.* Markus Wiener Publishers, 2003.

34. Levtzion and Spaulding.

    Diop, pp 118-120.

35. Burstein, pp 3-21.

    Heinemann, pp 117-186.

    McKissack, Patricia, and Fredrick McKissack. *The Royal Kingdoms of Ghana, Mali, and Songhay: Life in Medieval Africa.* Henry Holt and Company, LLC, 1995, pp 5-80.

36. McKissack, pp 43, pp56-57.

    Lvetzion, pp 60-64, 69-70.

    Heinemann, pp 640-672.

37. McKissack pp 108.

38. Diop, pp 64-65 (White Libyans); pp 49-50 (White Ethiopians); pp 43-45, pp133 (White Egyptians); pp 192-193 (White Carthaginians).

39. Diop, pp 43-84, pp 129-133, pp 149-151.

40. *Ainsley, Samantha. "Black Rhythm, White Power." The Morningside Review. Center for Digital Research & Scholarship: Columbia University Libraries/Information Services, 2007-2008 edition. www. morningsidereview.com*

41. *Abdul-Jabar, Kareem. "Cornrows and Cultural Appropriation: The Truth About Racial Identity Theft." Time, 26 August 2015. www.time.com*

42. *Madigan, Tim. The Burning: Massacre, Destruction, and The Tulsa Race Riot of 1921. Thomas Dunne Books, 2001, pp 3-6, pp 126-149.*

43. *Diop*. *(In its entirety)*

44. *Johnson, James Weldon. "Lift Every Voice and Sing." Saint Peter Relates and Incident: Selected Poems. Penguin Publishing Group. 1993, pp 101-102.*

REFERENCES

13th. Dir. Ava DuVernay. Netflix, 2016. Film.

A Special Presentation of American Experience: Eyes on the Prize: America's Civil Rights Movement, 1954-1985, PBS.org. Retrieved 2008. Documentary.

Abdul-Jabar, Kareem. "Cornrows and Cultural Appropriation: The Truth About Racial Identity Theft." Time, 26 August 2015. www.time.com

Ainsley, Samantha. "Black Rhythm, White Power." The Morningside Review. Center for Digital Research & Scholarship: Columbia University Libraries/Information Services, 2007-2008 edition. www.morningsidereview.com

Alexander, Michelle. The New Jim Crow: Mass Incarceration in the Age of Colorblindness. The New Press, 2012.

Baldwin, James. "A Talk to Teachers." The Price of the Ticket: Collected Non-Fiction 1948-1985. St. Martin's Press, 1985. (pp 325-332)

Bello, Marisol. "Mom of the Year? Baltimore Mom Isn't a Hero at All." USA Today, 29 April 2015. www.usatoday.com

Blackmon, Douglas A.. Slavery by Another Name: The Re-Enslavement of Black Americans from the Civil War to World War II. Anchor Books, 2009.

Burstein, Stanley. Ancient African Civilizations. 1st ed. Weiner, Markus Publishers, Inc. 2009.

Diop, Cheik A.. The African Origin of Civilization: Myth or Reality. Edited and translated by Mercer Cook. Lawrence Hill & Co., 1974.

Frieden, Jonathan D., and Leigh M. Murray. "The Admissibility of Electronic Evidence Under the Federal Rules of Evidence". Richmond Journal of Law and Technology, vol. 17, iss. 2, 2011.

Heinemann Educational Books. General History of Africa IV: Africa from the 12th to the 16th Century. Edited by D.T. Niane. United Nations Educational, Scientific, and Cultural Organization, 1984.

Johnson, James Weldon. "Lift Every Voice and Sing." Saint Peter Relates and Incident: Selected Poems. Penguin Publishing Group. 1993.

"Jumby." The Oxford English Dictionary. 2nd ed. 1989.

Katznelson, Ira. When Affirmative Action was White: An Untold History of Racial Inequality in Twentieth-Century America. Norton & Company, Inc., 2006.

Lawrence, Sarah, and Jeremy Travis. The New Landscape of Imprisonment: Mapping America's Prison Expansion. Urban Institute, 2004.

Levtzion, Nehemiah, and Jay Spaulding. Medieval West Africa: Views from Arab Scholars and Merchants. Markus Wiener Publishers, 2003.

Madigan, Tim. The Burning: Massacre, Destruction, and The Tulsa Race Riot of 1921. Thomas Dunne Books, 2001.

Marley, Bob. "Redemption Song." Uprising. Tuff Gong, 1980. CD.

Matthews-Whetstone, Rayna, and Joyce A. Scott. "Factors affecting bachelor's degree completion among Black males with prior attrition." Research in Higher Educational Journal, Volume 28, May 2015.

McKissack, Patricia, and Fredrick McKissack. The Royal Kingdoms of Ghana, Mali, and Songhay: Life in Medieval Africa. Henry Holt and Company, LLC, 1995.

Michel, Lawrence, and Jared Bernstein and Sylvia Allegretto. The State of Working America 2006/2007. ILR Press, 2007.

Morris, Monique W.. Black Stats: African Americans by the Numbers in the Twenty-first Century. The New Press, 2014.

Neubeck, Kenneth J, and Noel A. Cazenave. Welfare Racism: Playing the Race Card Against America's Poor. Routledge, 2001.

Oxford Dictionary of Quotations, 8th ed. Edited by Elizabeth Knowles. Oxford University Press, 2014.

Pager, Devah, Bruce Western, and Bart Bonikowski. "Discrimination in Low-Wage Labor Market: A Field Experiment." American Sociological Review, 2009, Vol. 74 (October: 777-799).

"Politically incorrect." The American Heritage Dictionary of the English Language. 5th ed. 2011.

Powell, John A., and Marguerite L. Spencer. "Giving Them the Old One-Two: Gentrification and the K.O. of Impoverished Urban Dwellers of Color." Berkeley Law Scholarship Repository, vol. 46 Howard L.J. 433, 2002.

"Punk." The American Heritage Dictionary of the English Language. 5th ed. 2011.

Stullich, Stephanie, Ivy Morgan, and Oliver Schack. State and Local Expenditures on Corrections and Education: A Brief from the U.S. Department of Education, Policy and Program Studies Service. July 2016.

The Associated Press. "Judge Has Sealed Alton Sterling's Autopsy Report, Coroner Says." NBC News, 2 August 2016.

The Bible. The KJV Study Bible. Barbour Publishing, Inc. 2011

Whitehead, John W., and Steve H. Aden. Forfeiting "Enduring Freedom" for "Homeland Security":A Constitutional Analysis of the USA PATRIOT Act and the Justice Department's Anti-Terrorism Initiatives. American University Law Review, vol. 51. The Rutherford Institute, 2002.

Woodson, Carter Godwin. The Mis-Education of the Negro. Digireads.com Publishing, 2016.

Woodson, Carter Godwin. The History of the Negro Church. The Associated Publishers, 1921.

Wright, Richard. Native Son. Perennial, 2003.

www.ingramcontent.com/pod-product-compliance
Lightning Source LLC
Chambersburg PA
CBHW071618040426
42452CB00009B/1383